THE BEST WINE BARS
& SHOPS OF PARIS

The Best
WINE BARS &
SHOPS of PARIS

By Pierrick Jégu

Photographs by Caroline Rose

Translated by Anita Conrade and David W. Cox

THE LITTLE BOOKROOM
NEW YORK

Originally published as *Aux Bons Crus,*
Les Meilleurs Cavistes de Paris
© 2007 Editions Parigramme, Paris, France
© 2007 Pierrick Jégu
Photographs © 2007 Caroline Rose
Translation © 2007 Anita Conrade and David W. Cox

Book design: Louise Fili Ltd.

Library of Congress Cataloging-in-Publication Data

Jégu, Pierrick.
[Aux bon crus, les meilleurs cavistes de Paris. English]
The best wine bars & shops of Paris / by Pierrick Jégu; photographs by Caroline Rose;
translated by Anita Conrade and David W. Cox.
p. cm.
Includes index.
ISBN 978-1-892145-63-5 (alk. paper)
1. Wine and wine making—France—Guidebooks. 2. Wine cellars—France—Paris—
Guidebooks. 3. Bars (Drinking establishments)—France—Paris—Guidebooks.
I. Title. II. Title: Best wine bars and shops of Paris.
TP559.F8J44 2008
641.2'20944361—dc22 2007044322

Published by The Little Bookroom
435 Hudson Street, 3rd floor
New York NY 10014
editorial@littlebookroom.com
www.littlebookroom.com
Distributed by Random House, Random House International,
and in the UK by Signature Book Services.

Printed in China

Contents

Introduction

T HE READER SHOULD NOT PRESUME TO FIND HEREIN YET ANOTHER ACCOUNT OF WINE'S HISTORY IN PARIS: THE vineyards of Montmartre, the riverside dance halls of Impressionist times, and the merry rumble of barrels on the cobblestones at Bercy, as whole bargeloads of wine were unloaded. No, the idea here is to take a contemporary photograph of Parisian wine cellars, and to set down in print and on film the most unusual wine-lovers' stops in the capital city. Since the mid-1990s, with new businesses being created and others closing, there has been a lot of turnover in the trade. It is constantly on the move, evolving and renewing itself. You will find establishments that have been serving for a century or two, neighborhood cellars, conventional purveyors, luxury houses, and hipster hangouts. A tour of Paris's wine cellars is an exploration of every state of mind, every age in history, and every consumer group. Likewise, from the traditional barrel on the sidewalk, the old-fashioned wooden cubbyholes for storing the bottles, rope-and-pulley dumbwaiters, creaking floorboards, and grumpy, mustachioed shopkeepers in starched white aprons, to ultramodern decoration schemes, sleek and streamlined design, vibrant wall colors, and waitstaff in jeans and sneakers, there is a broad spectrum of settings and moods to choose from. Moreover, beyond appearances, each cellar has its own approach, its own philosophy of wine, the products it swears by. One merchant may carry prestigious vineyards; a second, bargain *terroir* wines; the third, 100% organic libations; a fourth may offer fascinating

old vintages and finds for collectors, the cream of the French crop, but also beverages from afar. The variety is such that it is impossible to cover them all in one book, but this cross section of forty-nine reputable shops is an excellent map for those wishing to navigate the wine merchants of Paris.

Le Garde-Robe

41, RUE DE L'ARBRE-SEC, 1ST ARR.

☎ 01 49 26 90 60 🚇 LOUVRE-RIVOLI

CLOSED SATURDAY MORNING AND SUNDAY

PROPRIETORS CONTINUE TO PUN ON WINE-TASTING VOCAB-ULARY. AFTER LA ROBE ET LE PALAIS AND THE PRURIENT Dessous de la Robe, welcome to the Garde-Robe (the "robe" being the wine's appearance). Inside, you will enjoy more pungent vintner wit in an austere setting of wood and old stone. The storefront has a patina; the zinc counter will take you traveling back in time. A few tables in the back, a bouquet of flowers here, a mirror there, and shelves filled with bottles everywhere: all the ingredients of a charming and convivial Parisian

bistro. The benevolent institution has a penchant for healthful terrestrial nourishment, be it of the solid sort — check the blackboard for details about the delicious snacks — or the liquid, with a selection of amazing values from wine craftsmen and sought-after microclimates, such as Joblot vineyards Givry, Barral Faugères, or the extraordinary due-south beverage La Grange des Pères. Take it out or uncork it right there!

Lavinia

3, BOULEVARD DE LA MADELEINE, 1ST ARR.

☎ 01 42 97 20 20 · *www.lavinia.fr* 🚇 MADELEINE

CLOSED SUNDAY

FORGET THE CLICHÉ OF THE NARROW NEIGHBORHOOD WINE SHOP, CRAMMED WITH DUSTY BOTTLES FROM FLOOR boards to rafters. Lavinia is to the world of wine merchants what the skyscraper is to architecture: spacious, capacious, and monumental. The mammoth concept that gives rise to this big, beautiful wine shop happens to be the ambition to take in every possible latitude of the planet of vintners. A person could spend hours strolling the aisles of this 16,000-square-foot emporium, with its handsome, contemporary styling, absorbed in a detailed examination of the 3,000 superb samples of French wines stored in the basement, the 2,000 varieties of foreign wines lining the shelves of the street level, or shopping the 1,000 liqueurs and spirits displayed upstairs near the restaurant. These are dizzying figures, and the quality of the selection is also mind-boggling, one of its highlights being a premium collection of divine and truly grand *"crus"* stored in a special chilled case.

Lovin'

40, RUE SAINT-HONORÉ, 1ST ARR.

☎ 01 42 33 34 58 · *www.lovin.fr*

🚇 LOUVRE-RIVOLI OR LES HALLES

CLOSED SUNDAY AND MONDAY

WHEN IT OPENED ITS DOORS IN NOVEMBER 2003, THIS SHOP WAS ONE OF THE FIRST TO SHUN THE CONVENTIONAL cellar decor and opt for an avant-garde approach, splashed with bright white. This incarnation of the cellar is practically immaculate; the sign bears the subtitle: "*caviste contemporain.*" An original appellation, but the philosophy is anything but trendy and superficial. This knowledge-able cellar separates the fine wine from plonk, as a peek at its catalogue

will tell you. The Chablis wines by Jean-Marc Brocard, a vintner who is a friend/partner of the shop; the Languedoc labels La Tour Boisée and Le Domaine des Schistes; the Loire Valley's La Taille aux Loups; Montirius, grown in the Rhône region; and a selection of awesome Bordeaux (Cheval Blanc, Haut-Brion, Cos d'Estournel, etc.): all this is proof that, behind its ultra-modern façade, this cellar has the wisdom to offer an eloquent and enlightened choice.

Bernard Magrez

"COMPOSER OF RARE WINES": THE DESCRIPTION COULD BE WRITTEN ON THE BUSINESS CARD OF BERNARD MAGREZ, owner of some thirty-five vineyards throughout the world. Twenty are

located in the Bordeaux region, and there are others in Languedoc, Spain, Portugal, Uruguay, Argentina, Chile, and the United States. In need of a showroom where he could offer the 110 unique tasting experiences engendered by these grapes grown in so many different climates, Monsieur Magrez chose the heart of Paris, just around the corner from the Opéra Garnier. Feast your eyes on the precious woods, the shiny black façade, and the neo-baroque chandeliers designed by Philippe Starck. The shop looks more like

a luxury jeweler's than a neighborhood wine retailer. The walls are lined with the wines composed by the "maestro," standing at attention like soldiers. Admire a large-format photograph over the counter, showing horses drawing a plow on a plot in Pape-Clément, a reminder that, before it reaches the opulent surroundings of a fashionable shop, wine is a product of the soil.

Legrand Filles & Fils

1, RUE DE LA BANQUE, 2ND ARR.

☎ 01 42 60 07 12 · *www.caves-legrand.com* 🚇 BOURSE

CLOSED SUNDAY

I N THEIR GLORIOUS PAST, THE LEGRAND DAUGHTERS FAITH-FULLY SERVED GENERATIONS OF VINTNERS, GOURMETS, AND lovers of fine wine. Never fear, however; they're impervious to the ravages of age. This is not one of those historic shops on the decline, crumbling as time takes its toll. Les Caves Legrand reconciles the nobility of great ancestry and the freshness of a fashionable and up-to-date retailer. One side features a fine grocery, a dip into the sweet nostalgia of

a setting practically unchanged since 1880. The other, opening onto the magnificent Galerie Vivienne arcade, offers a choice of wines and dishes in a superb neoclassical decor, paneled in wood, and hundreds of beautifully classified bottles. Make a purchase to take home or have a taste at a table, accompanied by a first-class (but slightly pricey) snack. The inventory features the most noble offerings from France's vineyards, and could be a guide to its most amazing tasting experiences. Now, and no doubt for a long time to come, this engaging address will be peerless.

L'Estaminet d'Arômes et Cépages

MARCHÉ DES ENFANTS-ROUGES, 3RD ARR.

33 BIS, RUE CHARLOT

☎ 01 42 72 34 85 · *www.aromes-et-cepages.com*

🚇 FILLES-DU-CALVAIRE OR TEMPLE

CLOSED SUNDAY AFTERNOON AND ALL DAY MONDAY

IF YOU ARE FEELING IN NEED OF A BREAK FROM THE URBAN HUSTLE AND BUSTLE, HEAD FOR THE MARCHÉ DES ENFANTS-ROUGES. Founded in 1615, it is the oldest covered market in Paris, and when it re-opened in 2000, it became "the belly" of the Marais. It feels like a village square, with its colorful displays and basket-toting families and couples, browsing the pears and cheeses, the steaks and shrimp, the pasta and the pastillas. As the market's Mister Wine, Thierry Poincin is in charge of a

cheerful shop, offering the cream of the crop of the organic wine movement. Seated in his cozy and charming Estaminet, treat yourself to one
of the appetizing platters he composes. Relaxed, fun, and delightfully
tasteful, natural and devoid of pretentiousness, this shop is bound to win
you over with its friendliness, far from the madding and sometimes mad-
dening Parisian crowd. We recommend you arrange to meet a couple of
friends here, order a bottle of red (it's all good!) and a plate of *charcuterie*
or cheese. Enjoy the feast at one of the large wooden tables out front, as
you take in the spectacle of the market.

Julien, Caviste

IN THE EARLY 2000S, WINE CELLARS BEGAN POPPING UP IN THE NEIGHBORHOOD AROUND RÉPUBLIQUE-MARAIS-BASTILLE-Oberkampf, and the trend continues. Like many fellow retailers, Julien found a little shop to house his great passion and the wines he loves. Take a heap of old stones, a crumbling workbench standing in a corner, hang a painting or two on the wall, and add a splash of energy tempered by relaxation, and youthful flexibility. Of course, the vital ingredient, a bevy of attractive bottles, is on hand. That's his recipe for attracting shoppers eager for good advice and curious about new tasting experiences. This cellar does more than take you off the beaten track: the owners sniff out all manner of excellent finds. Our top recommendations are their Pouilly-Fuissé from Château des Rontets in Burgundy, Vincent Ricard's Touraines from the Loire, Ostertag treasures from Alsace, and the splendid Chermette Beaujolais. Above all, be sure to taste the peerless Château Roc de Cambes Côtes-de-Bourg.

Les Caprices de l'Instant

12, RUE JACQUES-CŒUR, 4TH ARR.

☎ 01 40 27 89 00 🚇 BASTILLE

OPEN SEVEN DAYS A WEEK

ANY CURSORY SURVEY OF THE HIGH SOCIETY OF PARISIAN CELLARS MIGHT MAKE THE MISTAKE OF OVERLOOKING THIS shop. After all, it is one of the few that do not clamor for attention with marketing and communications efforts. This merchant prefers to concentrate on his profession as a purveyor of fine wines. Yet the boutique is attractive, located in a quiet side street bordering the Marais and the Bastille, and offers all the verve, quality, and depth of the best. Don't come seeking prestigious labels; they are not the top priority here. What counts is the expression of the *terroir*, that mysterious combination of geology and microclimatology that finds all its eloquence in the proprietor's dis-

course, as well as in the vintages he makes available. From Bourgogne, Bordeaux, Alsace, the Languedoc, Loire and beyond, little gems and grand masters ensure that a visit will be well worth your while.

Les Caves du Marais

64, RUE FRANÇOIS-MIRON, 4TH ARR.

☎ 01 42 78 54 64 🚇 SAINT-PAUL

CLOSED SUNDAY AND MONDAY

RUE FRANÇOIS-MIRON, MEANDERING AS IT DOES BETWEEN HÔTEL DE VILLE AND SAINT-PAUL, PARALLEL TO RUE DE rivoli on the Seine side, houses some of the top gourmet addresses in Paris. At number 30, you will fine Izrael, one of the most fascinating exotic grocers in the city, a treasure trove of spices of the world. Number 80 is the address of The Auld Alliance, *the* Scottish pub of Paris, which, in addition to its collection of several hundred whiskeys, offers plenty of wit and entertainment. Between the two, at number 64, Jean-Jacques Bailly continues to fill his 430-square-foot shop with intriguing finds he gleans from the four corners of the vineyard. This bright, discreet little cellar contains crates and cartons just waiting to be opened, to reveal such clever bottles as the Temps des Cerises wines (Languedoc), Marcel Richaud's Cairanne, or the sparkle and pizzazz of Jacquesson champagne. A memorable stroll.

Cavestève

10, RUE DE LA CERISAIE, 4TH ARR.

☎ 01 42 72 33 05 · *www.cavesteve.com* 🚇 BASTILLE

CLOSED ALL DAY SUNDAY AND MONDAY MORNING

OLDER CONNOISSEURS MAY REMEMBER JEAN-MICHEL ESTÈVE AS THE "GURU" WHO INTRODUCED PARIS TO ORGANICALLY grown wines. At the time, the classically decked-out cellar set the standard and earned the respect of all Paris wine lovers, both amateur and professional. Now that the new owners have "remastered" the shop from top to bottom, it is difficult to recognize the venerable institution styled for the third millennium with extreme bareness and a virginal decor, all part of a quest for purity in design. The bottles are suspended in the shop

window like mobiles. Though there is a minority from elsewhere, the majority of the inventory is made up of French wines, especially unbeatable standards like Bollinger (Champagne), Chasse-Spleen (Moulis), Beaucastel (Châteauneuf-du-Pape) and Trimbach (Alsace). There are also some lesser-known labels: Arretxea (Irouléguy) and Lapalu (Beaujolais). Also worth a peek is the house grocery store/wine bar, just across the street.

Nysa

15, RUE DU BOURG-TIBOURG, 4TH ARR.

☎ 01 42 77 92 39 🚇 HÔTEL-DE-VILLE OR SAINT-PAUL

OPEN SEVEN DAYS A WEEK

WE WILL START WITH A HISTORY LESSON: ACCORDING TO GREEK MYTHOLOGY, MOUNT NYSA WAS THE PLACE where Dionysus, the alter-ego of the Roman god Bacchus, invented wine. The two young partners running this cellar may have gone back in time to find a unique name for their shop, which opened in 2006, but everything else about it is resolutely modern. The decor is Marais chic: contemporary, white, bare, and pure, with small boxes stuck to the walls to

display the bottles—the very opposite of the dusty-old-barrel and wooden-cubbyhole look. The approach to tasting is also original, shown in the form of stylized ideograms painted in red on the walls. Some sixty wines are offered, most notably among them the white Burgundy made by Emmanuel Giboulot. In terms of function, it may not be Paris's best cellar, but in terms of form, it is one of the most amazing.

Caves du Panthéon

174, RUE SAINT-JACQUES, 5TH ARR.

☎ 01 46 33 90 35   🚇 CLUNY-LA SORBONNE OR RER LUXEMBOURG

CLOSED ALL DAY SUNDAY AND MONDAY MORNING

THE LUXEMBOURG GARDENS ARE ON ONE SIDE, AND THE DOME OF THE PANTHÉON IS ON THE OTHER. BETWEEN THE two, a wine-lovers' monument: Les Caves du Panthéon. Though most travel guides make no mention of the shop, gourmets have long been aware of the pleasure potential of this Paris showroom. Long before the birth of the first *"appellation d'origine contrôlée"* (granted on May 15, 1936, to the Arbois wines from the Jura), these merchants had been preaching the fine wine gospel through many a grape harvest. Since then, time has spread a gentle patina over a lively and pleasing setting, while

the cellar continues to keep itself alert to vineyard sensations with an acuity that is rare and valuable. One of Paris's most tempting wine selections, alongside some gourmet grocery goods: that sums up the great merits of this bottle shop. Don't let your taste buds miss out.

De Vinis Illustribus

IF ERNEST HEMINGWAY RETURNED TO HIS OLD NEIGHBOR-HOOD, HE WOULD NO LONGER RECOGNIZE THE INDESCRIBABLE hodgepodge where he once bought his bottles. In those days, Jean-Baptiste Besse was the keeper of an incredible shop, a veritable jumble of vintages. It was said that legendary nectars and ambrosial flasks slumbered in the deepest reaches of the cellar, along with heaps of labels full of mystery and promise: the stuff of which dreams are made. In 2004, after a bit of tidying up (actually, it was a Herculean task!), Lionel Michelin created a sedate and seductive fine-wines venue, steeped in the comfort of bourgeois tradition. Although it has become rare to allow a wine to age, Michelin's taste buds long for such vintages. However, his love for the illustrious years, the wines which are now so rare, is that of an epicure, not a collector. The superb vaulted cellar, at the foot of the little stone stairway, attests to the wealth and expertise of this merchant. On the street level, you will find a small but eloquent selection of excellent everyday wines.

Les Papilles

30, RUE GAY-LUSSAC, 5TH ARR.

☎ 01 43 25 20 79   RER LUXEMBOURG

CLOSED SUNDAY

WHICH WINE MERCHANT WAS THE FIRST TO SET UP TABLES IN HIS CELLAR, TO SERVE CUSTOMERS FOOD ALONG WITH fine drink? That unknown soldier for the cause of sweet indulgence certainly had a stroke of genius that day. Today, shops where you can stock up on bottles and luxury eats are thriving. Their reservation books fill quickly, for the informal setting in which they accomplish their mission, filling stomachs with good food and the air with laughter and conversa-

tion, is an attractive concept. Here, elbow-to-elbow with the other diners, you will be tended to by a hale and hearty young man from southwestern France who trained at the four-star Bristol. Should you fall in love with a wine, you can take it home with you (and the offerings are good, great, and even sublime). You may also opt for such gourmet goodies as foie gras, sausages, jams, olive oils, and vinegars, all supplied by the finest sources.

Les Papilles

épicerie fine - cave à vins
vins de vignerons

ÉPICERIE n. f. Ensemble de denrées de consommation courante,
café, etc. / Commerce, magasin de l'épicier.

CAVE À VINS n. f. Boutique ou l'on vend des vins.

PETITE RESTAURATION n. f. Établissement public où l'on

TERROIR n.

Province, campagne, considérées so

La Crèmerie

9, RUE DES QUATRE-VENTS, 6TH ARR.

☎ 01 43 54 99 30 🚇 MABILLON OR ODÉON

CLOSED SUNDAY AND MONDAY

THE TINIEST CELLAR IN PARIS? IT MAY VERY WELL BE! THE SWEETEST? THERE IS NO DOUBT. AMERICAN VISITORS CAN be heard to murmur, "Charming," as they gaze, awestruck, upon this little shop paneled in marble and wood, with a superb ceiling dating from 1880, as attested by the plaque. The telephone is a 1940s model, and the impressive red Berkel (the meat-slicing machine) was made in 1936. "Delicious!" the same Americans no doubt exclaim, and everyone agrees, as they tuck into the outstanding snacks: a scrumptious *burrata*, Spanish deli meats that will knock you flat with amazement, a Parmesan aged thirty-six months seasoned with a few drops of balsamic vinegar, the salty/sweet sensation of dry chèvre and Cremona jam, and famed Utah Beach oysters from Normandy. And, to make the experience wholly sublime, they can be washed down with the finest natural wines. Take-out platters are available, as are oils, honey, jams, and vinegars. Serge and Hélène Mathieu offer jewel-like signature wines, such as Christian Ducroux's Régnié, Riffault's Sancerre, Fred Cossard's Saint-Romain, Hervé Souhaut's Ardèche wines, the Pic-Saint-Loup from Mas Foulaquier, and Les Griottes from Anjou...Thrilling!

55

La Dernière Goutte

6, RUE BOURBON-LE-CHÂTEAU, 6TH ARR.

☎ 01 43 29 11 62 🚇 MABILLON

CLOSED MONDAY MORNING

A FOREIGNER HAS MADE A FORAY INTO FRENCH TERRITORY... AN AMERICAN IN PARIS! HIS NAME? JUAN SANCHEZ. His art? Wine. His cellar? La Dernière Goutte, a narrow little shop with walls of old stone and wood paneling with the reassuring patina of age. Imagine an afternoon stroll through the neighborhood around St-Germain-des-Prés, peeking into art galleries and bookstores, designer boutiques, and student cafés. Imagine pushing open the wobbly door of number 6, rue Bourbon-le-Château.

Imagine hunting down rare and magical wines much like the precious old volumes you have just acquired at the used-book store. Imagine discovering an astounding selection of bottles from the most remote reaches of French wine-growing country, from Languedoc-Roussillon, to the Rhône Valley, to Burgundy, the Loire Valley, and Alsace. Imagine how delighted you will be. Okay, now wake up, it's true!

La Maison des Millésimes

137, BOULEVARD SAINT-GERMAIN, 6TH ARR.

☎ 01 40 46 80 01   🚇 MABILLON OR SAINT-GERMAIN-DES-PRÉS

OPEN SEVEN DAYS A WEEK

THE LIST IN LITTLE WHITE LETTERS ON THE WINDOW, ENUMERATING EVERY SINGLE ONE OF THE GIRONDE'S AOC wines, speaks for itself. Imported to Paris October 15, 2002, La Maison des Millésimes is nothing less than the embassy of Bordeaux wines. It concentrates on the production of a single region, the better to make an in-depth examination of it. On the Left Bank of the Seine, it presents the best of both banks of Bordeaux's River Gironde. There is no old wooden barrel on the sidewalk, the trademark of the old-fashioned cellar. This

merchant has no need to appeal to folklore to attract "Bordeaux addicts." Quite the contrary: in a streamlined setting paneled in light wood, the mood is one of discreet, contemporary elegance. The (diplomatic) mission is ambitious: they offer wines already aged to perfection, by means of 500 to 600 "*grand cru*" labels, a number of prized old vintage years from the famous vineyards, as well as the lesser known and less expensive producers.

La Quincave

17, RUE BRÉA, 6TH ARR.

☎ 01 43 29 38 24 🚇 VAVIN

CLOSED SUNDAY AFTEVRNOON AND ALL DAY MONDAY

IT MAY BE A SMALL CELLAR, BUT IT HAS LOADS OF PERSON-
ALITY AND IRRESISTIBLE CHARM. LOCATED IN A SPACE THAT
used to be a hardware store, it seems a bit like an antique shop at times,
with its huge baskets, old-fashioned furniture, bare wood, wine-making
tools, old wooden crates, and the funny lanterns hanging from the
rafters. It's a true neighborhood cellar, the one all of us wish was right

downstairs. You can poke your head
in, have a little chat, find a bargain
bottle, and, while standing at the
counter and munching on a bit of dry
sausage, taste the owner's latest find.
Just as simple as that. Engaging and
friendly, this shop has set its sights on
selecting the best wines from small
vineyards: Muscadet produced by
Landron, Bourgueil with the Breton
label, the Mâcon-Cruzille grown by
Alain and Julien Guillot, or Coteaux
Varois produced by Domaine du
Deffends. You will enjoy every visit.

Ryst-Dupeyron

79, RUE DU BAC, 7TH ARR.

☎ 01 45 48 80 93 🚇 RUE-DU-BAC

CLOSED ALL DAY SUNDAY AND MONDAY MORNING

"ESTABLISHED IN 1905, SPECIALIZING IN FINE WINES AND VINTAGE LIQUEURS, ARMAGNACS, PORT WINES, WHISKEYS, and champagnes"; so goes the story told on the brochure of this centenarian shop located in the seventh arrondissement. Behind the wood paneling of its façade, treasured by the historic building preservation trust, Ryst-Dupeyron welcomes wine-lovers to a velvety, posh cocoon with the impeccable courtesy and confidence belonging to a trusted old supplier of great quality. Without disdaining other wine-growing regions, the selection focuses chiefly on Bordeaux. It contains few surprises but a number of relevant items, including bottles from several famous châteaux and well-known labels of fairly recent vintages. The visitor can also explore a rare collection of old Armagnac brandies (going back to the late nineteenth century), intriguing whiskeys, a large range of Ports, and some of the most sparkling bubbly around.

Au Verger de la Madeleine

4, BOULEVARD MALESHERBES, 8TH ARR.

☎ 01 42 65 51 99 · *www.verger-madeleine.com* 🚇 MADELEINE

CLOSED SUNDAY

IT MAY INTEREST YOU TO KNOW THAT PIAF, GABIN, BLANCHE, AND VENTURA WERE ALL CUSTOMERS HERE. FOUNDED IN 1937 by a fellow named Legras, this pocket-sized cellar (193 square feet, to be exact), is definitely less bright and shiny than the world-renowned fancy grocers nearby at the Madeleine, but you may appreciate its discretion.

You will be in the company of some extremely well-informed customers, in terms of wine appreciation. From the secret caverns beneath this "orchard," a dumbwaiter from a bygone era retrieves bottled treasures: eye-popping rarities, legendary vintages, and some of the world's most sought-after wines and liqueurs. So, though it is tiny in terms of size, this cellar is enormous in scope; in addition to the Château Pétrus 1961 and the Armagnac-to-die-for, the merchant is talented enough to offer excellent wines at more affordable prices.

Caves Augé

"SINCE 1850": THAT'S WHAT IT SAYS ON THE AWNING OF THIS SHOP, WHICH PUTS IT IN A CLASS WITH THE OLDEST OF Paris's cellars. From this illustrious past, the premises have inherited an impressive "wine-merchant"-style interior, with superbly carved wood paneling, old-fashioned tiles, a magnificent dumbwaiter, and a cash register a museum would pay a fortune to own. The only concessions to changing times are a state-of-the-art computer and a credit card payment terminal. Despite the irresistibly obsolete charm of the shop, the wine selection ranks among Paris's most brilliant and alert. Constantly on the lookout for new finds, the house tasters continue to explore oenology, tirelessly traveling the vineyard route to compose an extraordinary catalogue for their customers. You will find the best of the natural wines, a few highly renowned producers, and an enviable collection of brandies and liqueurs.

Les Caves Taillevent

199, RUE DU FAUBOURG-SAINT-HONORÉ, 8TH ARR.

☎ 01 45 61 14 09 · *www.taillevent.com*

🚇 CHARLES-DE-GAULLE-ÉTOILE, TERNES, OR COURCELLES

CLOSED SUNDAY AND MONDAY

AUTHOR OF THE FIRST TREATISE ON FRENCH COOKING, THE FOURTEENTH-CENTURY CHEF GUILLAUME TIREL, ALIAS Taillevent, is the namesake of the world-famous restaurant, founded in 1946, and the establishment's cellar, which opened in 1987. As the creation of a wine-lover supreme, Jean-Claude Vrinat, Caves Taillevent bears his mark. It contains a spectrum of wines that is among the most brilliant the capital has to offer. To get an idea of the profundity of the cellar, simply leaf through one of the catalogues on the small stands in the shop or read the labels on the bottles lining the shelves. You will

immediately become aware you are in the presence of a master cellarman. In an elegant, distinguished setting, paneled in creamy wood, and in the "wings" of the cellar, thousands of bottles are aging: awe-inspiring vintages, true rarities, French wines as well as those from grapes grown around the world. And, lest we forget, the room called "Cave du Jour" houses a selection of forty more affordable, but no less exciting, wines.

Fauchon

SINCE 1885, THE NAME FAUCHON HAS BEEN INSEPARABLE FROM THE PLACE DE LA MADELEINE. AUGUSTE FAUCHON, A native of Normandy, began by selling fruits and vegetables from a push-cart in the market next to the church. By 1886, he settled there for good, opening a grocery store catering to luxury tastes. The rest is history: the shop quickly became a gourmet landmark. Obviously, it could not forget to put wine on the menu! In the basement, the cellar spreads out in a

space which is both pleasant and large enough to store nearly a thousand labels. Most of them are fairly upmarket, in terms of price and quality. The advice of an expert team of wine stewards brings in products from France and around the world: the great names in winemaking, legendary vineyards, rarities, and vintages ripe for rediscovery. But there are also many choices that, though less spectacular, are quite trustworthy.

La Maison du Whisky

20, RUE D'ANJOU, 8TH ARR.

☎ 01 42 65 03 16 · *www.whisky.fr* 🚇 MADELEINE

CLOSED SUNDAY

WE ARE TAKING A SLIGHT DETOUR FROM OUR PARISIAN WINE JOURNEY TO DISCOVER NEW HORIZONS. SCOTLAND, Ireland, Japan, Canada, and the United States are the five great whiskey-producing countries. This opulent and airy bottle shop, located a short walk from the Madeleine, can be your guide, teaching you everything you always wanted to know about whiskey but were afraid to ask: "MW" celebrated its fiftieth anniversary in 2006. A half-century of navigating the river of spirits has endowed it with the expertise to track down and acquire such a variety of liquor that it can claim to be the greatest specialist on the subject (in France at least). Blends, single malts, grain whis-

keys, bourbons: all the families, styles, schools, and nuances of the art are available here, in a selection that boasts more than a thousand references. Note that the shop has two branches, one on Réunion Island, and the other in Singapore. Bon voyage!

La Cave des Martyrs

BREAD MAESTRO ARNAUD DELMONTEL'S BAKERY IS NEXT DOOR; THE ADORABLE BRUNCH-SHOP, ROSE BAKERY, IS just opposite, and Molard's cheese shop is not far. In other words, this cellar fits perfectly into the "Gourmet Way" developing on rue des Martyrs. Under its previous ownership, the shop was called Tchin Tchin ("Cheers!"), and featured a blazing paint job and exciting wines. The current proprietor has toned down the color scheme and general mood of the store, but it is still an instructive guide to the products of French vineyards. By no means a fundamentalist, the cellarman is ecumenical enough to present a selection including Bordeaux grands *crus* (Lynch-Bages, Léoville Las Cases, etc.), the top-drawer in the bubbly market (Drappier, Jacquesson, etc.), as well as superb natural wines (De Moor Chablis, for example), and peerless *terroir* selections from small vineyards (Montpeyroux by Domaine Aupilhac). There is also a delightful choice of foreign wines (Domaine Torelli Moscato d'Asti). Excellent.

La Cave du Lafayette Gourmet

97, RUE DE PROVENCE, 9TH ARR.

☎ 01 48 74 42 93 🚇 HAVRE-CAUMARTIN OR
CHAUSSÉE-D'ANTIN-LA FAYETTE

CLOSED SUNDAY

FAR MORE THAN THE WINE DEPARTMENT OF A GOURMET SUPERMARKET, THIS IS A CELLAR IN AND OF ITSELF. ITS contemporary decor is quite pleasant, its ambience hums with excitement, and its selection will amaze you. Composed by Bruno Quenioux, whose wine knowledge is encyclopedic, the inventory claims to be a Library of Wines, endowed with some 3,500 listed wines. Naturally, the

number of labels is not always the best way to gauge a cellar's skills, but here, quantity, quality, and dynamics coincide to provide a panorama of wine production which is both broad and deep. Small alcoves are dedicated to each region, and the myriad signature wines, *terroir* labels, and sheer indulgences have been selected by the same palate. They may be ordinary *vins de pays* or premium *grands crus*; they may cost less than ten euros, or much more. Adjacent to all that, you will find a highly detailed range of liqueurs and a small wine bar. Conclusion? One of the capital's most enchanting cellars.

Le Verre Volé

67, RUE DE LANCRY, 10TH ARR.

☎ 01 48 03 17 34   🚇 JACQUES-BONSERGENT

OPEN SEVEN DAYS A WEEK

FEW LOCATIONS HAVE MORE PARIS "ATMOSPHERE" THAN THE CANAL SAINT-MARTIN AND THE LEGENDARY FOOT-bridge facing the Hôtel du Nord. Just a few steps away, you will find a food and wine cellar which has contributed as much to the renaissance of the neighborhood as to that of Paris's retail wine trade. It is the size of a postage stamp and just as colorful, with its assortment of used furniture, miniscule counter, bottle-lined walls, and few tables in the middle. Organized pandemonium characterizes this thimble-sized address which has had mammoth success. The honor is well-deserved, considering the fare, both liquid and solid, the house offers. Wines available on the premises or for takeout express the shop's 100%-natural preferences, with the best bottles in every category: white, red, and bubbly; healthful, amusing, unexpected, and gourmet. The snack menu, chalked onto a slate, includes a number of little marvels, room temperature or sensibly cooked: a sensational *andouillette*, *charcuterie*, cheese, *caillette pâtés*, and many other better-than-homemade dishes.

Aux Anges

30, RUE FAIDHERBE, 11TH ARR.

☎ 01 43 56 38 53   🚇 FAIDHERBE-CHALIGNY

OPEN TUESDAY-SATURDAY 4:30-8PM,

SUNDAY 5-10PM, CLOSED MONDAYV

EVIDENTLY, THIS PART OF THE ELEVENTH ARRONDISSE-MENT HAS A FEROCIOUS APPETITE! TAKE FOR EXAMPLE LE Paul Bert, a vibrant wine bistro; Unico, the Argentinean haven for meat-lovers; L'Écailler du Bistro, for seafood; Le Vieux Chêne with its decor honoring Bacchus. With all this, we are simply amazed that there was even a tiny little spot left for the delightful new cellar-eatery called Aux Anges. A showcase framed by huge windows, a counter that is deep

enough for cheese plates whipped up by Aléosse, a piano off in a corner, a bit of bric-a-brac, and cute little blackboards giving us the lesson of the day: Binner's White Alsatians (oh so fine), Collioure wines from La Tour-Vieille (remarkable), Stéphane Tissot's Jura production (excellent), and the Saumur-Champigny by Sébastien Bobinet (stupendous). Eat in or carry out. Your choice. Live music on Sunday evenings.

Cave de l'Insolite

FROM A DISTANCE, IT RATHER LOOKS LIKE AN ARTIST'S STUDIO ON THE CORNER OF A SLEEPY STREET AND A TYPICAL PARISIAN passageway. Close up, however, you will notice an assortment of bottles cleverly lined up at eye-level. Push through the shop's door and enter a haven of peace. Soothing. Relaxing. The horizontality of it all interrupted by an old spiral staircase. The walls are built in noble freestone. Different and very charming. This wine shop is unusual for its warm yet uncluttered ambience, and for its selection of bottles from vineyards which refuse to be grandiose. Plain, healthy, good drink made purely from the fruit of the fields is favored here. Whether Loire, Languedoc, Rhône Valley, Beaujolais, or other stock, the shopkeepers here know the alphabet of natural vineyards by heart. Natural? Yes, you know, from wine growers who make their wine from grapes, and grapes alone. The kind who labor and tend to their own vines, the kind who refuse to tamper with the fermentation process. Their produce is within reach: fine table wines and spirited labels.

91

La Muse Vin

THE DEFINITION OF *CAVE À MANGER* IS A PLACE WHICH SELLS BOTTLED WINE FOR CARRYOUT BUT THAT ALSO SERVES food on the premises and where bottles on display may be sampled for a pop-the-cork price (generally between five and seven euros). In the space of a few short years, the phenomenon has mushroomed in certain Paris quarters such as the eleventh arrondissement. This wine merchant is part of the movement and has a nice approach to it. As a wine shop with

attitude, this youngster thumbs its nose at the snobbish old blathering on wine. Here, it is talk about enjoyment, and nothing but! What is the shop like? A shocking pink façade, bright colors, a little counter, tables in the middle, and bottles all around, to drink or takeout? An ABC of natural wines, with little or no sulfur, unfiltered, often very good, sometimes astounding, all produced by French vineyards. The food? Clever plates with a neo-bistro ring.

Le Baron Rouge

STAND WATCHING THE CROWD HERE WASH BACK A DOZEN OYSTERS OUTSIDE ON A WINTRY SUNDAY, AND YOU WILL SEE that this charming bistro can look forward to many more fine years. Located in the Aligre market area, the Baron Rouge is a monument. Plates of *charcuterie* and cheese platters are whisked to tables. Waiters with dish towels on their shoulders stand behind the bar. Glasses of wine slide across the zinc countertop. Clusters of friends clamor to buy rounds of drinks. The owners' wine specials are scrawled on a blackboard. Gents from the neighborhood pop in for a glass of wine poured directly from a spouted keg. A very merry and very varied clientele – that's the Baron Rouge in a nutshell. Granted, the place is more a wine bar than a wine shop. And of course, persnickety wine buffs can find "better" elsewhere (frankly, though, the wines served here are nothing to sneeze at). Be that as it may, 1, rue Théophile-Roussel deserves its place in this guide for its spirit and its sensitivity.

MERLOT
d'Ardèche
vin de pays 12°
le litre 2.80

MERLOT
d'Ardèche
vin de pays 12°
le litre 2.80

CÔTES
DU
RHÔNE
Dom. le Garrigon
à Tulette, Drôme
2005 BIO
le litre : 4.20

BEAUJOLAIS nouveau
michel Guignier
à Villié Morgon
6€ le litre

La Cave du Square

1, RUE ANTOINE-VOLLON, 12TH ARR.

☎ 01 43 43 65 91 🚇 LEDRU-ROLLIN

CLOSED SUNDAY AND MONDAY

SURELY YOU HAVE BEEN BY THE HUNDRED-YEAR-OLD BISTRO NAMED SQUARE TROUSSEAU? IT OPENED THIS WINE shop just next door in 1998. If you loved a wine served at table, you can buy it here when the restaurant is open and serving. Chock-full of old-fashioned charm, it can seat fifteen comfortably. The floorboards are warped. The literature is gastronomic. Salted meats and copper cookpots hang from old meat hooks. The cuisine? Flawless bistro-style meals. Convivial and efficient service. The wines? Natural. Lapierre representing

Beaujolais, Pacalet and Valette from Burgundy, Binner produced in Alsace, Overnoy from the Jura Mountains, Barge and La Vieille Julienne from the Rhône Valley, Cousin from the Loire Valley, Château Meylet from Bordeaux. Want a tip? Reserve the place for an evening for a dozen or so friends. Start by heading down the small, rickety stairs to enjoy a drink in the basement, which you will find as intimate and inviting as an alcove.

102

Rouge, Blanc et Bulles

12, RUE PARROT, 12TH ARR.

☎ 01 43 47 45 14   🚇 GARE-DE-LYON

CLOSED ALL DAY SUNDAY AND MONDAY MORNING

RED, WHITE AND BUBBLY, BUT ALSO EXPECT ROSÉS, SPIRITS, AND EVEN BOTTLED WATER (THE SAINT-GÉRON IS A naturally sparkling water from Auvergne). This pretty and modern wine shop is run by energetic young people who go for the gusto. The shop sets a wide and remarkable spread for its group wine tastings. If the owners like a vintage, it will find its place in the shop's catalogue. It is as simple as that. As a result, the place is crammed with bottles from floor to ceiling. Two hundred excellent champagnes (Jacquesson, Krug, Bollinger, Alexandre L, and Roses de Jeanne, to name but a few), hundreds of wines in all three colors like Roc de Cambes from Côtes-de-Bourg, Ostertag from Alsace, Gauby from Roussillon, Haut-Marbuzet from Saint-Estèphe, Mas Jullien from Languedoc, Gramenon from the Rhône, Taille-aux-Loups from Montlouis, and the list goes on. From good to very good to excellent to rare if you look beneath the tip of the iceberg and take a trip downstairs.

L'Avant-Goût Côté Cellier

37, RUE BOBILLOT, 13TH ARR.

☎ 01 45 81 14 06   🚇 PLACE-D'ITALIE

OPEN DAILY FROM NOON, CLOSED SUNDAY AND MONDAY

IF THERE WERE EVER A CHAMPIONSHIP FOR THE TINIEST PARISIAN WINE SHOP, THIS ONE WOULD LIKELY WIN THE GOLD. Call it the thirsty-little-sister of the bistro-like and delicious Avant-Goût, the restaurant across the street. The specialty? Trendy natural wines, but nothing too extreme. Preference goes to wines characteristic of their native soil and bearing the mark of exceptional winemakers like Thierry Michon (Fiefs Vendéens), Robert Plageoles (Gaillac), or tender young wines like those produced by Yannick Pelletier (Saint-Chinian) and Anne-Sophie Debavelaere (Rully). There is not a single false note in this spirited score which is necessarily well-honed, given the limited space. Despite the tight squeeze, a few of the shelves offer a selection of gourmet delights (oils, vinegars, gingerbread). Be sure to check the little refrigerator for carryout delicacies cooked up by Christophe Beaufront, the fine chef and owner of the restaurant.

La Cave des Gobelins

56, AVENUE DES GOBELINS, 13TH ARR.

☎ 01 43 31 66 79 🚋 LES GOBELINS OR PLACE-D'ITALIE

CLOSED SUNDAY AND MONDAY

VINTAGE 1922. THIS SHOP IS ONE OF THE GRANDDADDIES OF PARISIAN WINE SHOPS. IT HAS SEEN MANY SHOPS OPEN AND many wine merchants close their doors. Unlike numerous contemporaries, this business is still here, standing on the gently sloping avenue, completely at ease encased in its dated storefront, proud of the old map of French vineyards drawn on its façade. At a time when new wine shop owners opt for trendy twenty-first-century design, this shop holds fast to its turn-of-the-previous-century decor, its old woodwork, and all the courtesies of our elders. Antiquated and quaint. So, naturally, the offer is rather classic, nothing too avant-garde here. On the other hand, the stock is neither musty nor outdated. You may expect excellent advice and directions to such trusted labels as Clos Marion and Bruno Clair among the Burgundies, Schlumberger among the Alsatians, and Domaine de Veilloux if you want a taste of Touraine.

La Cave des Papilles

35, RUE DAGUERRE, 14TH ARR.

☎ 01 43 20 05 74   🚇 DENFERT-ROCHEREAU
OR MOUTON-DUVERNET
CLOSED SUNDAY AFTERNOON AND ALL DAY MONDAY

RUE DAGUERRE...STILL ONE OF THE CITY'S POPULAR STREETS WITH OLD-TIME ARTISANS, CAFÉS, RESTAURANTS, FOOD shops galore, and one of the best wine shops on the Left Bank. On the corner, the yellow-and-plum storefront's lettering reads, "Cave des Papilles, successeur des Caves Saint-Vincent" (literally: "The Taste Bud Wine Shop, previously St. Vincent Wines"). The ambience leans to the bohemian and artsy side of things. A few paintings hang on the walls. The sales staff know their stuff and show more interest in good (and we mean very good) organic wines than prestigious labels. They know all the ins and outs of natural vineyards, cherishing the wine growers who respect the nature of the fruit and the lay of the land, whether they be in the Rhône Valley, the Loire Valley, in Languedoc, in Roussillon, in Burgundy, Alsace or elsewhere. Among their "faves" are Schueller who produces magnificent Rieslings and Gewurztraminers, Allemand's Rhône Valley vineyards in Cornas, Barral and his Faugères, and Simonutti with his remarkable Touraine production.

110

Les Crus du Soleil

WHILE MOST WINE SHOPS TRY TO PROVIDE A HEALTHY SAMPLING OF ALL OF FRANCE'S APPELLATIONS, THE monomaniac Crus du Soleil bucks the trend and positions itself as the embassy of Languedoc-Roussillon wines. Serge Lacombe and his pals continue to promote the fantastic evolution in quality in this wine-growing region. They make frequent trips back and forth between Paris and "down there" bringing back bottled treasures to maintain their absolutely brilliant stock. Unless you are planning to hop on a train to Montpellier, Béziers, or Perpignan, we advise you to saunter over to the fourteenth arrondissement to feel the winds of the South and admire a Pic-Saint-Loup, a Minervois, a Collioure, or maybe a Corbières. The

action takes place in a lovely wine shop where the gift of gab is never squandered! Warm, sunny yellow walls, a stunning historic ceiling, black-and-white shots of vineyards, scattered books, sausages hanging off in one corner, and the table in the backroom of the shop certainly looks set for guests.

La Treille d'Or

21, RUE DE LA TOMBE-ISSOIRE, 14TH ARR.

☎ 01 45 80 35 49 🚇 SAINT-JACQUES

CLOSED ALL DAY SUNDAY AND MONDAY MORNING

"I LIKE WINES THAT YOU CAN DRINK, WINES THAT STAY SMOOTH, LIGHT, EASY ON THE STOMACH." THIS IS NICOLAS Sirieix's profession of faith, or taste, rather. Translation: his shop does not carry any wines that are overrated or pretentious, contest winners, overpowering nectars, bottles that knock your taste buds, head, or stomach out of commission at the first sip. In his basic wine shop, with a map of

wine-producing regions in one corner, a few books in another, and a wine cask in the middle, he braids laurel wreaths for several sublime natural wines made by growers who are "capable of producing interesting things at each vintage." He praises Jean Foillard (Morgons), Bénédicte and Grégoire Hubeau (Château Moulin-Pey-Labrie, Canon-Fronsac), Dominique Derain (Burgundy), Thierry Navarre (Saint-Chinian), Guy Jullien (Domaine de la Ferme-Saint-Martin, Rhône) and Thierry Puzelat (Touraine). Because he is fond of them, he is meticulous in how he describes them. His wine cellar is kept at a constant 14°C (57°F), and his air-conditioned shop is kept at a constant wine-friendly temperature.

Cave à Millésimes

180, RUE LECOURBE, 15TH ARR.

☎ 01 48 28 22 62 · *www.cave-millesimes.com* 🚇 VAUGIRARD

CLOSED SUNDAY AND MONDAY

LOCATED ON ONE OF THOSE INCREDIBLY LONG STREETS CUTTING ACROSS THE FIFTEENTH ARRONDISSEMENT, THIS IS one place which seems to have no particular distinction. Exterior view? Huge store windows, a folding screen, the name of the shop spelled out in big red letters on a gray background. Interior view? Your standard wine-shop decor, very organized, everything lined up, like a model student's desk. The view of the bottles? Ah, here is where this shop differs from most of the competition. While the others are quenching their thirst with young wines, this shop travels back in time and puts a spotlight on old and rare vintages. A Château Margaux 1995? Coming right up! An Yquem 1995? No problem. A Château Ducru-Beaucaillou 1961? Ditto that. Of course, the Bordeaux and the Burgundies count for much of the inventory, but other regions are not slighted, far from it. You will find the old and the new of them.

La Cave de l'Os à Moelle

181, RUE DE LOURMEL, 15TH ARR.

☎ 01 45 57 28 28   🚇 LOURMEL

CLOSED MONDAY

LOCATED IN THE HEART OF PARIS, YET THE FEEL IS SO DIF-FERENT...THIS PLACE IS LIGHT YEARS FROM THE USUAL Parisian ambience. It offers the warmth of a country inn, the conviviality of bistros of yesteryear, and knows wine like nobody's nose. Admire the magnificent but tiny counter, the brick walls, the wooden crates, the stout stove in the middle of the room, the sturdy tables laden with delicious terrines and home-cooked delicacies. This is a place after your heart. They can whip up a fine meal for you and your friends for a price so decent it will conjure up a bygone era. And the drink will take you down

the paths wine growers know. The food here is genuine and true. Feel free to drop by any time of the day to pick up a bottle and choose from over one hundred natural wines. Flawless!

Le Goût des Vignes

12, RUE LAKANAL, 15TH ARR.

☎ 01 42 50 00 33 🚇 COMMERCE

CLOSED ALL DAY SUNDAY AND MONDAY MORNING

THIS IS THE STORY OF A YOUNG CHAP WHOSE PASSION FOR WINE BLOSSOMS IN THE ROWS OF VINES AND IN A COUPLE of excellent vineyards. This is the story of the same strapping lad who decides to share his experience and his favorites with Parisians by opening shop on a little street in the 15th arrondissement. In 2003, he opened his own business in a place barely as wide as an apartment hallway. Naturally, there is no getting around the cardboard boxes and stacks of bottles. Though the space is tiny, its success has been phenomenal! At rush hour, customers may have to stand in line outside before being admitted to the inner sanctum. The stock includes the great standards, but people really come here for the extra special little wines, great finds originating from vineyards all over the globe. A few privileged spots have been made for bottles from Burgundy, the Rhône Valley, and Languedoc. You may be interested in knowing that "hands-on" lessons may be had during one of the shop's wine-tasting dinners.

Le Nez Rouge

11, RUE ALEXANDRE-CABANEL, 15TH ARR.

☎ 01 47 34 18 64   🚊 CAMBRONNE

CLOSED SUNDAY AND MONDAY

IS IT "NEZ ROUGE" OR "RED NOSE" LETTERED ON THE SHOP WINDOW? IT IS ANY WAY YOU LIKE IT. IT ALL DEPENDS ON the language you prefer to use at the moment, for this wine shop is not the sort to be concerned with borders, even less by blind patriotism to defend French wines. This shop loves them, of course; half its catalogue is devoted to a selection of truly remarkable domestic products like Montlouis by Grange-Tiphaine, Fronton-labeled Le Roc, and so on. The cellar also features foreign wines (made from indigenous varietals). Unlike many competitors, your trusty shopkeeper here has tasted them on site in Italy, South Africa, Portugal, Argentina, Switzerland, the United States. Since 1996, the Red Nose has had a global view of wines. We expect the shop will continue surprising our palates and introducing us to new horizons. The decor? Ultra basic, nothing frilly. A few photos here and there of foreign vineyards.

Aux Caves de Passy

3, RUE DUBAN, 16TH ARR.

☎ 01 42 88 85 56　🚊 LA MUETTE

CLOSED SUNDAY AND MONDAY

TWO, THREE, OR—HEAVEN FORBID—FOUR PERSONS COMING THROUGH THAT DOOR AND SUDDENLY THE SHOP IS FULL. Only Philippe Charmat knows his way through the crates and boxes artfully piled up, creating semblances of alleyways. Magazines and guidebooks are strewn here, there, and everywhere. The stocked shelves appear almost tidy. It is a bit (!) of a mess, rather nonchalant, yet endearing at the same time. This straightforward wine shop can nevertheless boast a couple of wagon loads of very fine stuff. The owner has many a trick up his sleeve: remarkable everyday wines, new bottles fresh off the press, mature vintages, as well as greats sure to please label-chasers. It is a veritable hodgepodge. Dig around a bit and you will notice Philippe Valette's Mâcon-area wines, the Givry produced by Joblot, the Saumur-Champigny from Clos Rougeard, the Creisses and the Mas Cal Demoura from Languedoc, Lynch-Bages and the Château Brande-Bergère from the Bordeaux region, and lots of other incredible vintages.

Les Grandes Caves

IN THE CITY OF CLICHY SINCE 1946, IN PARIS FOR AGES, TOO. THEY HAVE SHOPS ON RUE SAINT-DOMINIQUE (7TH), RUE DAMRÉMONT (18th), rue de l'Annonciation (16th), and rue Poncelet (17th). For sixty years, Les Grandes Caves and its "offspring" have garnered a solid reputation as a chain. Their success lies in plying strong skills. An institution. There! The word has been uttered! Here you will find none of the usual layer of dust that covers the shelves of declining businesses. Les Grandes Caves retains a youthful, perky, wide-awake attitude; they're undoubtedly some of the best wine shops in the capital. For example, head over to rue Poncelet. While the neighboring produce seller hawks his luscious fruits and vegetables, the wine shop, with its reassuring decor, keeps customers quite content.

Over 1,100 items from all regions, particularly from Burgundy (Gros, Engle, Dugat-Py, Jobard, etc.), the Loire Valley, the Rhône Valley, and Languedoc-Roussillon.

Le Vin en Tête

RUE DES BATIGNOLLES HAS A WELL-ESTABLISHED REPUTATION FOR FOOD SHOPS, AND THANKS TO LE VIN EN TÊTE, the street has been saved from thirst. Every day, neighborhood residents' admiration for this shop's team grows a little more. The young, dynamic, and enterprising staff knows how to satisfy customers' curiosity. There is a fun poster with photos of all the active members of this charitable group, decor with lots of red, a bit of white, a touch of black and some old stone. So much for the wrapping. Organic wine, biodynamic *crus*, natural wines, some "a tad more conventional," always lots of high-quality stuff. That describes the superb selection. Keen, combative, and geared for new experiences, the stock includes the battle-worn and the new recruits. The stock is quite simply remarkable. There is also an assortment of gourmet foods. You may wish to top off your shopping with oenology classes. Wine Tasting 101 takes place only a few yards away at a nearby wine bar called Oh Bigre!

Les Caves du Roy

31, RUE SIMART, 18TH ARR.

☎ 01 42 23 99 11 🚇 JULES-JOFFRIN

CLOSED ALL DAY SUNDAY AND MONDAY MORNING

PARTY-PEOPLE BEWARE: THIS PARIS WINE SHOP IS NOT TO BE CONFUSED WITH THE LEGENDARY ST. TROPEZ CLUB OF the same name. It is totally different, and we mean totally. Jean-Luc Tucoulat is not the type who goes for glam, sequins, or artifice. Since 1986, this dedicated wine merchant has plied his trade in the most earnest way. His quest has been to be as meticulous with his wines as he is with his concern for the value triad of quality-price-pleasure, and, in the end, customer satisfaction. What is the shop like? It is located on a little street near the eighteenth arrondissement City Hall and has an old-fashioned

storefront. Once you cross the threshold, you find yourself in a small but warm wine shop chock-full of bottles. There is a fascinating selection of wine from all French vine-yards. Behind the counter is an array of liquors that is much more interesting than standard fare.

Chapeau Melon

92, RUE RÉBEVAL, 19TH ARR.

☎ 01 42 02 68 60 🚇 PYRÉNÉES

CLOSED SUNDAY MORNING AND MONDAY

TABLE D'HÔTE FROM WEDNESDAY TO SATURDAY

HE HAS BEEN SPOTTED AT LE BARATIN, A NEIGHBORING BISTRO KNOWN FOR ITS GREAT FOOD AND WINES. HE HAS been seen advising several restaurants on improving their wine lists. Now he is back again on the slopes of Belleville. "He" is none other than Olivier Camus, a pioneer in natural wines, a talent scout, a discoverer of domaines, a brilliant palate for unfiltered, no-sulfate, 100%-grape wines. Hats off to Chapeau Melon ("melon" being the grape variety used to make Muscadet), and especially to Monsieur Camus for piecing together a lovely ambience for his wine shop, for his suave blend of yesterday and today, something between art deco and outsider art. He deserves credit for continuing to feature pure pleasure wines (and much more than that : Mosse, Binner, Lemasson, Derain, Gramenon, Petit Domaine de Gimios, Foulards Rouges, etc.). He deserves praise for cooking up those delicious and outstanding dishes to be tasted on the tables in the middle of the shop or at the counter.

Ma Cave

105, RUE DE BELLEVILLE, 19TH ARR.

☎ 01 42 08 62 95   🚇 PYRÉNÉES OR JOURDAIN

CLOSED SUNDAY AFTERNOON AND ALL DAY MONDAY

THE STRETCH OF THE RUE DE BELLEVILLE BETWEEN MÉTRO STATIONS PYRÉNÉES AND JOURDAIN IS ONE OF THE MOST endearing shopping areas of Paris. It naturally lends itself to strolling, shopping basket in hand, picking up groceries. Fruit, vegetables, meats, fish, bread, pastries...there is a full menu to be had on the sidewalks of this street. So be sure you stop in regularly at Ma Cave (literally: My Cellar). For nearly fifty years, this has been the neighborhood's main purveyor of wines. This shop always has excellent bottles and is always thronged with happy customers who know they have come to the right address. From floor to ceiling, in little boxes painted red or yellow, in crates crowding the already limited space, bottles and still more bottles, illustrious unknowns and grandiose wines alike, prestigious labels and anonymous vintages. All of them have been selected with great care for a demanding clientele. This is a neighborhood wine shop, and so much more.

Caves Au Bon Plaisir

104, RUE DES PYRÉNÉES, 20TH ARR.

☎ 01 43 71 98 68 🚇 MARAÎCHERS

CLOSED SUNDAY AFTERNOON AND ALL DAY MONDAY

THIS PLACE HAS A DISTINCTIVE AURA OF BYGONE DAYS. OLD CERAMIC TILES, WORN EARTHEN FLOOR TILES, WOODEN crates that bottles have been sleeping in for who knows how long. The venerable shop gives you the impression it has not changed one iota since it opened roughly a century ago in 1910. Today's owners perpetuate its vocation as a convivial, warm, generous neighborhood shop with a distinctive stock of products from around France. What are the house favorites? Wines from Languedoc-Roussillon and the Rhône Valley, but it does not slight other regions. Although this is a liquids shop, its second staple

is regional products like terrines and foie gras. Sausages from Mont Gerbier de Jonc are laid out on a counter in a pretty wooden crate. Here is one wine shop that can grow on you. It is now affiliated with the neighboring wine bar À La Vierge de La Réunion.

Other Recommended
Wine Bars and Shops

JUVENILE'S
47, rue de Richelieu, 1st arr. ☎ 01 42 97 46 49
🚇 Pyramides or Palais-Royal-Musée-du-Louvre

A Scottish owner, a sky-is-the-limit cuisine, wines from everywhere, the most international of Parisian bistros cum wine shops. It is certainly not the least frequented!

BACCHUS ET ARIANE
4, rue Lobineau, 6th arr. ☎ 01 46 34 12 94
www.bacchus-ariane.com 🚇 Mabillon

Located in the Marché Saint-Germain. An excellent selection of wines. Tables in the arcades for a bite to eat out of doors.

DA ROSA
62, rue de Seine, 6th arr. ☎ 01 40 51 00 09 🚇 Mabillon or Odéon

Gourmet grocer and fine wines. Meals served.

VINS ET COLLECTIONS
117, rue du Cherche-Midi, 6th arr. ☎ 01 42 22 86 92 🚇 Falguière

A cozy wine shop. Nice bottles ranging from your daily pleasure to very fine *grand crus* classés.

CAVE DE LA GRANDE ÉPICERIE

38, rue de Sèvres, 7th arr.   ☎ 01 44 39 81 00

www.lagrandeepicerie.fr   🚇 Sèvres-Babylone

Perhaps not terribly "sexy," but it is one of the most reliable wine shops in Paris.

LES GRANDES CAVES

70, rue Saint-Dominique, 7th arr.   ☎ 01 47 05 69 28

🚇 La Tour-Maubourg or Invalides

The finest wine shop in the 7th? Perhaps it is!

NOÉ, L'ANTIQUAIRE DU VIN

12, rue Malar, 7th arr.   ☎ 01 47 05 01 02

www.antiquareduvin.com   🚇 La Tour-Maubourg or Invalides

Specializes in wines from the eighteenth century to today. A veritable treasure chest!

LE CHEMIN DES VIGNES

7, rue Pasquier, 8th arr.   ☎ 01 42 65 39 86

🚇 Saint-Augustin or Madeleine

A good address for lunch. Wonderful wines for takeout can be purchased all day.

DE LA VIGNE AU VIN

55, boulevard des Batignolles, 8th arr.   ☎ 01 53 04 00 33   🚇 Villiers

A small, inconspicuous wine shop that aims to give you rock-solid value for your money.

LE VIN EN TÊTE – SAINT-GEORGES

48, rue Notre-Dame-de-Lorette, 9th arr. ☎ 01 53 21 90 17

🚇 Saint-Georges

A small shop with leading *terroir* wines, made with methods that respect the fruit and the lay of the land.

AU NOUVEAU NEZ

112-114, rue Saint-Maur, 11th arr. ☎ 01 43 55 02 30 🚇 Parmentier

A tiny wine shop offering big-name natural wines. What else? Little plates of food if you would like to pull up a barstool.

CRUS ET DÉCOUVERTES

7, rue Paul-Bert, 11th arr. ☎ 01 43 71 56 79 🚇 Faidherbe-Chaligny

Just a hop and a skip from the fabulous bistros on rue Paul-Bert. The selection is up-to-date and with it.

LES DOMAINES QUI MONTENT

136, boulevard Voltaire, 11th arr. ☎ 01 43 56 89 15 🚇 Voltaire

22, rue Cardinet, 17th arr. ☎ 01 42 27 63 96 🚇 Malesherbes

A lovely shop with a good selection of wines. What's makes this shop special? Lunch served up *table d'hôte* style. Very convivial.

LE VERRE VOLÉ

38, rue Oberkampf, 11th arr. ☎ 01 43 14 99 46 🚇 Oberkampf

This is the daughter shop of the one in the tenth arrondissement. A lively shop purveying the leading natural wines.

CAVE MICHEL RENAUD

12, place de la Nation, 12th arr.   ☎ 01 43 07 98 93   🚇 Nation

An institution. Venerable vintages, legendary bottles, a collection of Armagnac, reasonably-priced table wines. Something for every taste and budget.

CHAI 33

33, cour Saint-Émilion, 12th arr.   ☎ 01 53 44 01 01

www.chai33.com   🚇 Cour-Saint-Émilion

Three in one: shop, restaurant, bar. A sleek XXL decor. Located in Bercy's old wine warehouse block. Delights for carryout or immediate consumption.

LES CRUS DU SOLEIL

21, rue d'Aligre, 12th arr.   ☎ 01 43 43 52 20   🚇 Ledru-Rollin

The best of Languedoc and Roussillon, just like at the older shop of the same name in the fourteenth arrondissement.

LE VIN SE LIVRE

38, allée Vivaldi, 12th arr.   ☎ 01 43 40 59 45

🚇 Montgallet or Daumesnil

Two in one: wine shop and bookshop. Original, isn't it? A brief but witty selection of natural wines.

CAVE BALTHAZAR

16, rue Jules-Guesde, 14th arr.   ☎ 01 43 22 24 45

www.cavebalthazar.com   🚇 Gaîté

Unassuming and contemporary. A wine shop where they know domestic and international fine wines by heart.

LE COMPTOIR DES ANDES 3

19, rue Delambre, 14th arr.   ☎ 01 43 20 03 00   🚇 Edgar-Quinet

A pocket-sized shop with an original selection that is 100% Chilean. Friendly, fun, warm!

MI-FUGUE MI-RAISIN

36-38, rue Delambre, 14th arr.   ☎ 01 43 20 12 06   🚇 Edgar-Quinet

Unheard of! Two passions: one boutique. Classical music with some very fine record labels, and wine with a stupendous selection from the organic trend. Outstanding.

CAVES DARGENT

45, rue de Vouillé, 15th arr.   ☎ 01 40 45 09 10

www.cavesdargent.com   🚇 Plaisance

An appropriate decor and a well-defined catalogue. From amazing finds to guaranteed values.

COULEURS DE VIGNE

2, rue Marmontel, 15th arr.   ☎ 01 45 33 32 96

🚇 Vaugirard or Convention

A pleasant address, both wine shop and bistro. Carry it out or pop the cork in the store. Lovely wines from all regions. Its plus point? Charming service.

LES PETITS BOUCHONS

105, rue Cambronne, 15th arr.   ☎ 01 47 34 89 31

🚇 Vaugirard or Volontaires

Far better than a neighborhood wine shop, a lively cellar with a hefty selection and a friendly, hospitable owner!

LES GRANDES CAVES

38, rue de l'Annonciation, 16th arr. ☎ 01 45 25 80 97 🚇 La Muette

The newbie among Les Grandes Caves. As sharp as the others!

LA CAVE 106

106, rue Cardinet, 17th arr. ☎ 01 43 80 21 25 🚇 Malesherbes

Go for Jean-Pierre Descaves's favorites. The man has a great sense of taste!

LES GRANDES CAVES

63, rue Damrémont, 18th arr. ☎ 01 53 41 06 77

🚇 Lamarck-Caulaincourt or Guy-Môquet

As remarkable as its sister wine shops.

LA PALETTE DES VINS

185 bis, rue Ordener, 18th arr. ☎ 01 42 64 20 38 🚇 Guy-Môquet

A historic wine shop in this neighborhood. A palette of high-caliber wines, a wide range of prices.

Wine Bars and Shops Serving Food

Index